CAMP,

GARRISON AND GUARD DUTY,

WITH A MODIFIED

MANUAL OF ARMS

FOR THE

OFFICERS AND SOLDIERS

OF THE

MICHIGAN INFANTRY.

BY W. W. DUFFIELD,

COLONEL NINTH MICHIGAN INFANTRY.

DETROIT:

PUBLISHED BY WM. B. HOWE.

FREE PRESS PRINT.

1861.

CAMP,

GARRISON AND GUARD DUTY,

WITH A MODIFIED

MANUAL OF ARMS

FOR THE

OFFICERS AND SOLDIERS

OF THE

MICHIGAN INFANTRY.

BY W. W. DUFFIELD,

COLONEL NINTH MICHIGAN INFANTRY.

DETROIT:

PUBLISHED BY WM. B. HOWE.

FREE PRESS PRINT.

1861.

Headquarters Ninth Regiment Michigan Infantry,
FORT WAYNE, October 1, 1861.

THE following little pamphlet has been hastily arranged for the use of the officers and soldiers of the Ninth Regiment of Michigan Infantry, and is intended as a Field Book of ready reference upon the most common and every day duties of the officer and soldier.

If it will enable them to acquire a knowledge of their duties, at a less expenditure of time and study, than has been incurred by their brethren already in the field, the labor necessary to its compilation will not be regretted by

Their Friend and Fellow Soldier,

WM. W. DUFFIELD.

CAMP AND GARRISON DUTY.

The calls most common in camp are as follows:

1. REVEILLE. This is the signal which awakens the soldier at day break.

2. PEAS ON A TRENCHER. This is the signal for breakfast.

3. FIRST SERGEANT'S CALL. This is the signal which brings the First Sergeant of each company to the Adjutant's quarters. It is used for bringing in the morning reports, to notify the First Sergeants of the issue of rations, or any detail necessary to be attended to by them in camp.

4. SICK CALL, sometimes called *Surgeon's call,* is the signal for bringing invalids to the hospital.

5. TROOP. Is the signal for guard mounting.

6. ROAST BEEF. Is the signal for dinner.

7. ADJUTANT'S CALL. (The first part of the Troop,) is the signal for the Adjutant to come for orders. It is also the signal for assembling companies for dress parade on the battalion parade ground.

8. RETREAT. This is usual at sunset, and is the signal for firing the sun down gun.

9. TATTOO. This is the signal for retiring to quarters.

10. TAPS. This is the signal for extinguishing lights. Upon the drum it is a seven stroke roll and nine taps; upon the bugle it is No. 12 of U. S. Infantry Tactics of 1861.

11. ASSEMBLY. This is the signal for the companies to assemble on their company parades.

12. TO THE COLOR. This signal forms the battalion. It usually succeeds the assembly.

13. THE DRUMMER'S CALL. This signal brings the drummers together for beating the stated calls.

These calls for the fife and drum can be found at the close of the first volume of Scott's Infantry Tactics; for the bugle in U. S. Infantry Tactics of 1861, pp. 194-214.

There are three daily roll calls in each company, under the superintendence of one of its commissioned officers. The first follows immediately after reveille, the second after retreat, or evening parade, and the third immediately after tattoo. Absentees from either roll call, unless excused, are usually subjected to extra tours of guard, or police duty.

Immediately after reveille roll call the tents and quarters are put in order by the men in each company, under the superintendence of the chiefs of squads. The guard-house or tent is put in order by the guard, or when sufficiently numerous, by the prisoners.

The morning reports of each company, signed by its Captain and First Sergeant, will be handed into the Adjutant daily, at the First Sergeant's call, and consolidated by the Adjutant for the Colonel's information.

At the sick call, (or Surgeon's call,) the sick then in the companies are conducted to the hospital by one of the Sergeant's, (the First when practicable,) who will each hand to the Surgeon, in his company book, a list of all the sick of the company, on which the Surgeon will state who are to remain in, or go into hospital; who are to return to quarters as sick or convalescent; what duties the convalescent in quarters are capable of; what cases are feigned, and any other information in regard to the sick of the company he may have to communicate to the company commander.

GUARD MOUNTING.

Camp and garrison guards are relieved every twenty-four hours.

The first call for guard mounting is usually the assembly. It precedes the second call, which is the troop, fifteen minutes. At the first call, the men warned for duty turn out on their company parades for inspection by the First Sergeant of each company. At the second call, they repair to the regimental parade, conducted by the First Sergeant. Each detachment as it arrives, will, under the direction of the Adjutant, take post on the left of the one that preceded it, in open order, arms shouldered, and bayonets fixed, the First Sergeants in rear of the men of their respective companies. The Serjeant-Major will dress the ranks, count the files, verify the details, and when the guard is formed, report to the Adjutant, and take post two paces on the left of the front rank.

The Adjutant then commands *Front*, when the officer of the guard takes post twelve paces in front of the centre; the Sergeants of the guard (but not the First Sergeants) in one rank, four paces to the rear of the officer, and the Corporals in one rank, four paces in rear of the Sergeants, all facing to the front. The music is formed in two ranks on the right of the line. If there is a junior officer of the guard, he takes post twelve paces in front of the centre of the fourth section, as if he were a First Lieutenant. The Adjutant then assigns their places in the guard. This is usually done by supposing the guard to constitute a company, of which the officer of the guard is Captain, the junior officer (if there be one) is First Lieutenant, and the Sergeants, First, Second and Third, according to seniority. Thus the officer of the guard will be assigned to the command of the first platoon, the junior officer to the command of the second platoon, the senior Sergeant will be guide of the first platoon, and the next in rank the guide of the second platoon, etc.

The Adjutant will then command,

1. *Officers and non-commissioned officers.* 2. *About*—FACE! 3. *Inspect your guards*—MARCH!

At the second command the officers, Sergeants and Corporals, face about; at the third command they take the posts assigned them, except the officer of the guard, who stands fast, after having faced about, and commands,

1. *Order*—ARMS! 2. *Inspection*—ARMS!

And inspects his guard. When there is a junior officer of the guard, he inspects the rear rank, and when there is no commissioned officer on the guard, the Adjutant will inspect it. During inspection the band will play.

The inspection ended, the officer of the guard takes post four paces in front of the front rank of the guard opposite his post on the right. The junior officer will take post four paces in front of the front rank, opposite the centre of the fourth section. The officers of the day will, at the same time, take post in front of the centre of the guard. The old officer of the day three paces on the right of the new officer of the day, and one pace retired.

The Adjutant will now command,

1. *Parade*—REST! 2. *Troop*—BEAT OFF!

When the music beginning on the right will beat down the line in front of the officer of the guard to the left, and back to its place on the right, where it will cease to play.

The Adjutant now commands,

1. *Attention.* 2. *Shoulder*—ARMS! 3. *Close Order*—MARCH!

At the words "close order," the officers will face about; at "march" resume their posts in line.

The Adjutant then commands,

Present—ARMS!

He will then face to the officer of the day, salute, and report, "*Sir, the guard is formed.*" If the Adjutant is of higher rank than the officer of the day, he will report without saluting, either then, or when marching in review. The new officer of the day, after acknowledging the salute, will direct the Adjutant to march the guard in review, or by a flank to its post.

If in review, the Adjutant will then face about and command,

1. *By platoon, right wheel.* 2. MARCH! 3. *Pass in review.* 4. *Column forward.* 5. *Guide right.* 6. MARCH!

The guard marches in review past the officer of the day, officers saluting, and conducted by the Adjutant, who marches on the left of the first platoon, the Sergeant-Major on the left of the last platoon.

When the column passes the officer of the day, the Adjutant, Sergeant-Major, and First Sergeants, retire, and the officer of the guard marches it to its post. The music marches at the head of the column until it arrives opposite the officer of the day, where it wheels out of the column, and takes post opposite the officer of the day. When the rear of the column has passed, the music will cease. The old officer of the day will then salute the new officer of the day, and transmit to him the orders and the instructions he may have received, and under which he has been acting as officer of the day, during his tour of service the day previous.

The old officer of the guard, on the approach of the new guard, forms his old guard in line, and taking post on its right commands,

Present—ARMS!

The new guard marches past the old in quick time, at *shouldered arms*, officers saluting and takes post four paces on its right, where, having formed on the same line with it, the new officer of the guard will command,

Present—ARMS!

The two officers will then approach each other and salute. They will then return to their respective guards, and both command,

1. *Shoulder*—ARMS! 2. *Order*—ARMS!

The new officer of the guard having ascertained from the old the number of posts, will divide his guard into three reliefs, make out the list of his guard, and will proceed to take possession of the guard-house or guard-tent, and the articles and prisoners in charge of the guard, and while the sentinels are being relieved, the old officer of the guard will give to the new all information and instructions he may have received during his tour of service.

The first relief is designated and marched two paces to the front. It is then numbered, the numbers beginning with the right front rank man, who is number one, the right rear rank man being number two, the front rank man of the second file from the right being number three, and so on alternately from front to rear and right to left. A Corporal of the new guard will then take charge of the first relief, and proceed to relieve the sentinels of the old guard still on post, accompanied by a Corporal of the old guard, who will take command of the old sentinels when the old are relieved.

If the relief consists of more than twelve sentinels it will be commanded by a Sergeant, if of twelve, or less, sentinels, by a corporal.

The relief will march by a flank in two ranks, with arms constantly at the support. The first relief being numbered, the Corporal in charge of it will command,

1. *Without Doubling, Right*—FACE! 2. *Support*—ARMS!
3. *Forward.* 4. MARCH!

While on the march should an officer approach, the Corporal will comand *shoulder arms*, and bring his relief again to *support arms* when the officer has passed.

The sentinel at the guard tent will be number one, and will be the first relieved, the others will be successively relieved in their numerical order.

When a sentinel sees the relief approach in the day time, he will halt and face to it with his arms at a shoulder. At six paces from him the Corporal will command,

1. *Relief.* 2. HALT!

When the relief will halt and bring its pieces to the shoulder without further orders. The Corporal will then command, according to the number of the post,

Number one, (or two, or three,) Arms—PORT!

Both old and new sentinels will then take the position of *arms port*, and approach each other; the old sentinel whispering to the new the orders and instructions he has received relative to his post. The Corporal will see that such orders are properly communicated by the old sentinel to the new one. Both sentinels will then shoulder arms, the old sentinel passing in quick time to his place in rear of the relief, the new sentinel remaining at his post.

1. *Support*—ARMS! 2. *Forward.* 3. MARCH!

And the relief proceeds in the same manner until the whole is relieved.

When all the sentinels of the old guard have been relieved and brought in, the old officer of the guard will march his guard in quick time past the new guard, the old guard carrying their pieces at a *shoulder*, the new standing at *presented arms*, both officers saluting, and the drums of both guards beating.

Before the old guard is dismissed, their pieces will be drawn or discharged at a target.

When the old guard has marched off fifty paces, the officer of the new guard will order his men to stack their arms, and will then make himself acquainted with all the instructions for his post, visit the sentinels, and question them, as well as the non-commissioned officers, relative to the instructions they may have received from other persons of the old guard.

In brigade encampments the officer of the day must be a field officer, but in regimental encampments there is a daily detail of a Captain to act as officer of the day, a First Lieutenant to act as officer of the guard, and a Second Lieutenant to act as officer of police. The detail of non-commissioned officers and privates for the guard will be published daily in battalion orders. The Adjutant will furnish to the Sergeant-Major the detail, and the Sergeant-Major will furnish to each First Sergeant the number of non-commissioned officers and privates to be detailed from each company. This will be given to the First Sergeants on tickets, immediately after evening dress parade, and the men detailed for the morrow's guard will be notified by the First Sergeant, on or before tattoo roll call.

The soldier detailed to act as orderly will not be placed on post as a sentinel, but will report for orders to the Adjutant immediately after guard mounting, and attend at head-quarters from 8 o'clock A. M., till 6 o'clock P. M.

OFFICER OF THE DAY.

The officer of the day, during his tour of service, is the immediate commander of the encampment, under the directions of the Colonel or commanding officer, and is charged with its good order and cleanliness. His authority embraces the entire encampment. A fatigue is furnished him when necessary. He will see that the regular calls are beaten at the proper time by the drummer of the guard. The drummer of the guard is usually the drummer of the company commanded by the officer of the day.

Immediately after the old guard is marched off, the new officer of the day will report for orders either to the commanding officer, or to such person as may be designated by him for that purpose, usually the Lieut. Colonel.

He will see that the officer of the guard is furnished with the parole and countersign before twilight. He visits the guards during the day at such times as he may deem necessary, and ascertains from the sentinels their orders and instructions.

During the night he will satisfy himself frequently of the vigilance of the guard, and himself make the rounds at night, at least, once before and once after midnight.

Upon being relieved, he will make such remarks in the report of the officer of the guard as circumstances require, and present the same at head-quarters.

OFFICER OF THE GUARD.

This officer in regimental encampments is usually a First Lieutenant. He is subordinate to the officer of the day, and will obey all orders received from him. He will remain constantly at his post, at or near the guard-tent, unless while visiting his sentinels, or necessarily engaged elsewhere in his proper duty. Upon leaving his post, he will mention his intention and probable time of absence to his immediate subordinates, the officer of police, or Sergeant of the guard.

Neither officers or soldiers will take off any of their clothing or accoutrements, or retire to their quarters while on guard, but hold themselves in constant readiness at the guard-tent, at all hours of the day and night, during their entire tour of duty.

The officer of the guard must see that the countersign is communicated to the sentinels a little before twilight. During the night, he orders patrols and rounds to be made by the officer of the police and Sergeant of the guard, whenever he thinks necessary, and himself visits the sentinels frequently. Patrols are made usually after the sentinels have been on post an hour, or intermediate to the relief.

He will make a report of his tour of service according to the form prescribed by regulation, and when relieved forward it to the officer of the day.

OFFICER OF POLICE.

The officer of police will be subordinate to the officer of the guard, and will aid and assist him in his duties. He will have the immediate superintendence of the police guard during his tour of service, and all police duty about the encampment. The sentinels of the police guard, and all interior guards, are not provided with the countersign.

The sword and sash will be worn by officers of the day, guard, and police, during their entire tour of service. The sash will be worn by officers of the day across the body, from the right shoulder to the left hip, instead of round the waist.

SENTINELS.

Sentinels should be relieved every two hours, unless the weather renders it necessary to shorten their duty on post.

Each relief, before mounting, is inspected by the officer of the guard. The Corporal, or Sergeant in command of the relief reports to him, and presents the old relief on his return.

The countersign is given to such persons as are entitled to pass during the night, and to officers, non-commissioned officers, and sentinels of the guard.

The parole is imparted to such officers only as have the right to visit the guards and to make the grand rounds, and to officers commanding guards.

In brigade encampments the parole is imparted to general officers; in regimental encampments it is usually given to field officers.

When a fire breaks out, or any alarm is given in camp, all guards are to be immediately under arms.

Sentinels will not take orders, or allow themselves to be relieved, unless by an officer or non-commissioned officer of the guard, the officer of the day, a general or field officer, or the commanding officer. All orders given to sentinels by any officer of higher rank than the officer of the guard, will be immediately notified to him by the officer giving them.

Sentinels will report every breach of orders or regulations they are instructed to enforce.

Sentinels must keep themselves on the alert, never sitting down while on post, but observing everything that takes place within sight and hearing of their post. They will carry their arms habitually at a support, or on either shoulder, but will never quit them, or allow them to be examined or taken out of their possession by any person whatever. In wet weather they will secure arms.

No sentinel will quit his post, or hold conversation with any persons not necessary to the proper discharge of his duty. If circumstances require a temporary relief, he must call for the Corporal of the guard, and be regularly relieved.

All persons, of whatever rank in the service, are required to observe respect toward every sentinel.

In case of disorder, a sentinel must call out *the guard*. If a fire breaks out, he must cry "*Fire*," adding the number of his post. If in either case the danger is imminent, he must discharge his piece before calling out.

Each sentinel must repeat all calls made from posts more distant from the guard-tent than his own, and no sentinel will be posted so distant as not to be heard by the guard, either directly or through other sentinels. Thus, the sentinel on post No. 9, upon hearing the call, "Corporal of the guard No. 10," must repeat the call in the same words, "Corporal of the guard No. 10," and this call will be repeated in succession by the sentinels at posts Nos. 8, 7, 6, 5, 4, 3, 2, and 1. By this means, the Corporal of the guard is not only notified of the demand made upon him, but of the precise locality where his presence is required.

Sentinels will *present arms* to general and field officers, to the officer of the day, and the commanding officer, although of a rank below a field officer. To all other officers they will *shoulder arms*, having previously brought their pieces to the support arms, prior to the officer's approach. Sentinels are instructed to present arms to all officers who have two rows of buttons upon their coats, or the sash worn across their bodies; to all other officers they shoulder arms from the support.

The sentinel at any post of the guard, when he sees a body of troops or an officer entitled to compliment approach, must call out the guard, and announce who approaches. Thus, on the approach of the commanding officer, he would call; "*Turn out the guard; commanding officer!*" when the guard is paraded, and salutes with presented arms. In active service this rule, however, is somewhat modified as to the commanding officer, who is entitled to the same compliment as the officer of the day, on his approaching the guard-tent.

In the day time, when the sentinel before the guard-tent sees the officer of the day approach, he will call: "*Turn out the guard; officer of the day!*" The guard will be paraded and salute with presented arms.

Sentinels present arms to all bodies of troops under the command of a commissioned officer; to those in command of a non-commissioned officer they will shoulder arms from a support.

Guards do not turn out, as a matter of compliment, after sunset, and no compliments will be paid by sentinels after that hour, other than those prescribed for grand rounds.

After the countersign is issued, until broad day light, sentinels will challenge every person who approaches them, bringing their pieces to arms port. They will not come to the charge bayonet, unless the person challenged continues to advance after the order to halt. They will not fire, unless three successive challenges are passed unnoticed, or unless they are attacked.

A sentinel in challenging calls: "*Who comes there?*" If answered: "*Friend with the countersign,*" and he is instructed to pass persons with the countersign, he will reply: "*Advance friend with the countersign.*" If answered: "*Friends with the countersign,*" he will reply: "*Halt friends; advance one with the countersign.*" This rule is absolute and imperative. The sentinel must never allow more than one person to approach him. Thus, if his challenged is answered, "*relief,*" or "*patrol,*" or "*grand rounds,*" he will reply: "*Halt relief,*" or "*patrol,*" or "*grand rounds, advance Corporal.*" or "*Sergeant with the countersign,*" and satisfy himself that the persons or party are what they represent themselves to be. If he have no authority to pass persons with the countersign, or a wrong countersign be given, or the persons have no countersign whatever, he will cause them to stand and call: "*Corporal of the guard,*" adding the number of his post. The sentinel will compel every person to advance to him and give the countersign, and never advance himself for the purpose of receiving it.

It is a safe rule, after dark, to compel every person to enter or leave the camp by the guard tent, whether they have the countersign or not."

When any person approaches the guard tent at night, the sentinel before the guard tent, after challenging, causes him to halt until examined by a non-commissioned officer of the guard. If it be the officer of the day, or any other officer entitled to inspect the guard and to make the grand rounds, the non-commissioned officer will call: "*Turn out the guard,*" and announce who approaches, when the guard will be paraded at shouldered arms, and the officer of the guard will, if he thinks necessary, demand the countersign and parole.

The officer of the day, or any other officer authorized to do so and wishing to make the grand rounds, will take from the guard an escort of a Sergeant and two men. When the rounds are challenged by a sentinel, the Sergeant will answer: "*Grand rounds,*" and the sentinel will reply: "*Halt grand rounds; advance Sergeant with the countersign.*" The Sergeant then advances alone and gives the countersign. The sentinel will then call: "*Advance rounds,*" and stand at a shoulder till they have passed. After having made the tour of the camp and arrived once more at the guard tent, when the sentinel before the guard tent challenges and is answered: "*Grand rounds*" by the Sergeant of the escort, the sentinel will reply: "*Halt grand rounds; turn out the guard, grand rounds,*" upon which the guard will be drawn up at shouldered arms. The officer of the guard then directs a Sergeant and two men to advance. When within ten paces, this Sergeant challenges. The Sergeant of the grand rounds answers: "*Grand rounds.*" The Sergeant of the guard replies: "*Advance Sergeant with the countersign.*" The Sergeant of the rounds advances alone, gives the countersign, and returns to his round. The Sergeant of the guard calls to his officer: "*The countersign is right,*" on which the officer of the guard calls: "*Advance rounds.*" The officer of the rounds then advances alone, the guard standing at shouldered arms. The officer of the rounds passes along the front of the guard to the officer, who keeps his post on the right, and gives him the parole.

In brigade encampments any general officer, or the commanding officer of a regiment, may visit the guards of his own command, and go the grand rounds, and be received in the same manner as prescribed for the officer of the day. In regimental encampments any field officer of the regiment is entitled to the same privilege.

All material instructions given to a sentinel on post, by persons entitled to make grand rounds, ought to be promptly notified to the officer of the guard, by the persons giving such instructions.

DRESS PARADE.

There will be daily one dress parade at *troop* or *retreat*, as the commanding officer may direct.

Half an hour before *troop* or *retreat*, a signal will be beaten or sounded, (usually *the assembly*) for the music to assemble on the regimental parade, and each company to turn out under arms on its own parade, for inspection and roll call by its own officers.

Ten minutes after that signal, the *Adjutant's call* will be given, when the Captains will march their companies (the band playing) to the regimental parade, where they take their positions in the order of battle as follows: The color company takes its position first, under the direction of the Adjutant. This company will throw out both right and left guides, and be aligned by its Captain by the right. This captain will then step into the rear rank of his company, to allow the Captain of the company on the right of the color to align his company by the left. The first Sergeant of the color company will take post in the line of file closers opposite his interval. As soon as the color company is aligned by its Captain, the company on the left of the color will take its position in line. Its left guide will place himself on the alignment of the guides of the color company, so as to be opposite one of the three left files of his company. Its Captain will then align his company by the right. The company on the right of the color will then take its position, its right guide placing himself upon the alignment of the color guides, so as to be opposite one of the three right files of his company. Its Captain will then align his company by the left. The other companies will then form successively to the right and left, the Captains of the left wing throwing out their left guides, and aligning their companies by the right, and the Captains of the right wing throwing out their right guides, and aligning their companies by the left. The guides, as they place themselves upon the alignment, will bring their pieces to the present. The Adjutant seeing the battalion in line, will command

Guides—POSTS,

when the guides will resume their positions in line, passing for this purpose through the nearest Captain's interval; the Captains of the right wing, who are on the left of their companies, shifting to the right, passing by the front rank, and the Captain of the color company will step into the front rank, and be covered by his First Sergeant. The Adjutant will then command

Present—ARMS,

when arms will be presented, officers saluting.

The Adjutant will then face about to the commanding officer, salute, and report: "*Sir, the battalion is formed.*"

The commanding officer, having acknowledged the salute by touching his cap, will draw his sword and command,

1. *Battalion.* 2. *Shoulder*—ARMS.

He will then return his sword and direct the Adjutant to form the parade.

The Adjutant then takes his post two paces on the right of the line, the Sergeant Major two paces on the left. The music will be formed in two ranks on the right of the Adjutant. The Captain of the first company, on notice to that effect from the Adjutant, steps one pace to the front, faces to the left, and gives to his company the command

1. *First Company.* 2. *Order* ARMS. 3. PARADE REST,

and retires to his post on the right of his company. This is repeated by each Captain in succession, from right to left. Each Captain will describe his company by its number, as "second company," "third company," etc.

The ceremony will then proceed in accordance with the form as prescribed in army regulations.

All field and company officers and men will be present at dress parade, unless specially excused, or on some duty incompatible with such attendance.

At the last word of the command "PARADE REST," the soldier will carry the right foot six inches in rear of the left heel, the left knee slightly bent, the body upright upon the right leg, the musket resting against the hollow of the right shoulder, the hands crossed in front, the backs of them outward, and the left hand uppermost. In this position the soldier will remain silent and motionless, not turning the head or changing the position of the feet. At the command "ATTENTION" the soldier will resume the position of ordered arms.

The officers, at the command "PARADE REST," will reverse the sword, rest the point on the ground in front of and between the feet, clasp the left hand over the right, both resting on the guard, and carry the right foot six inches in rear of the left heel, the left knee slightly bent, the body upright upon the right leg. At the command "attention," they will raise the sword smartly, place the back of the blade against the right shoulder, bring the right heel upon the line of the left, and stand erect.

Beating the Calls.

The drummer's call will be beaten by the drummer of the guard five minutes before the time for beating the regular calls, when the drummer of each company will take post on the color line, in front of his own company's street. As soon as the beat begins on the right, it will immediately be taken up along the line. For reveille and tattoo, however, all the drums and fifes will assemble on the right of the color line, and as the call is beaten, the field music will march through the different company streets.

For an hour previous to tattoo, the band will play in front of headquarters.

MANUAL OF ARMS.

In order to adapt the Rifle Manual of the U. S. Infantry Tactics of 1861 to the musket, it will be necessary to modify it in the following particulars. In all other particulars the manual of arms for the rifle will be adhered to.

LOAD IN NINE TIMES!

1. Load.

One time and two motions.

First Motion. Carry the right foot forward, placing its heel against the hollow of the left, but without altering the position of the body. At the same time seize the piece with the left hand at the middle band, detaching it slightly from the shoulder.

Second Motion. Quit the piece with the right hand, and with the left hand carry it obliquely across the body, and bring it to the ground without shock, resting it against the left thigh, rammer to the rear, butt outside of and against the left foot, muzzle opposite to and three inches from the center of the breast. Carry the right hand to the cartridge box and open it.

2. *Handle*—CARTRIDGE.

One time and one motion.

Take the cartridge between the thumb and first two fingers and place the end in the teeth.

3. *Tear*—CARTRIDGE.

One time and one motion.

Tear the end of the cartridge down to the powder, holding it upright, and place it in front of or near the muzzle, the back of the hand to the front.

4. *Charge*—CARTRIDGE.

One time and one motion.

Empty the powder into the barrel, and if a musket is used, insert the cartridge in the barrel. If a rifle, lower the right hand near the left, disengage the ball from the paper with the right hand and the thumb and first two fingers of the left. Insert it in the bore, the pointed end uppermost, and press it down with the right thumb. Seize the head of the rammer with the thumb and forefinger of the right hand, the other fingers closed, the elbows near the body.

5. *Draw*—RAMMER.

One time and three motions.

First Motion. Draw the rammer by extending the right arm; seize it again at the middle between the thumb and forefinger, palm of the hand to the front, the nails up, the fingers extended and joined; clear the rammer entirely by again extending the arm, the rammer in the prolongation of the pipes.

Second Motion. Turn the rammer between the bayonet and face, by closing the fingers, the rammer parallel to the bayonet, the arm extended, the butt of the rammer near the muzzle, but not yet inserted.

Third Motion. Insert the rammer and force it down as low as the hand, turning the hand as it comes down, so that the back of the hand may be to the front, the elbow down and near the body.

6. *Ram*—Cartridge.

One time and one motion.

Extend the arm to its full extent, seizing the rammer between the right thumb extended and the forefinger bent, the other fingers closed, press the ball home with force, the back of the hand to the front, the elbow down and near the body.

7. *Return*—Rammer.

One time and three motions.

First Motion. Draw the rammer by extending the right arm; reseize it at the middle between the thumb and forefinger, palm of the hand to the front, the nails up, the fingers extended and joined; clear the rammer from the barrel by extending the right arm, the rammer in the prolongation of the barrel.

Second Motion. Turn the rammer between the bayonet and the face by closing the fingers, the rammer parallel to the bayonet, the arm extended, the little end of the rammer near the first pipe, but not yet inserted.

Third Motion. Insert the rammer as far as the hand; raise the right hand, placing the little finger on the butt of the rammer and force it down, and lower the left hand on the barrel to the full extent of the arm, without depressing the shoulder.

8. PRIME.

One time and three motions.

First Motion. Bring up the piece vertically to the left shoulder with the left hand, seize it with the right hand at the small of the stock, and slide the left hand down as low as the chin.

Second Motion. Make a half face to the right, as in *about face*, except that the hollow of the right foot is close against the left heel, instead of three inches to the rear, carry the piece opposite to the right shoulder, bring it down by the right side with both hands, the left thumb extended along the stock, the butt under the right forearm, the small of the stock against the body, the right thumb on the hammer, the fingers under and against the guard.

Third Motion. Half cock the piece, brush off the old cap with the thumb, carry the hand to the cap box, observing if any smoke comes from the tube, (a certain indication that the piece has been fired,) take a cap between the thumb and first two fingers of the right hand, place it firmly on the cone, pushing it down with the thumb, and seize the piece by the small of the stock.

9. *Shoulder*—ARMS.

One time and two motions.

First Motion. Face to the front, turning on the left heel, bring the right foot alongside of the left; bring the piece to the right shoulder, right hand embracing the guard between the thumb and forefinger, slip the left hand to the height of the shoulder, the fingers extended and joined.

Second Motion. Drop the left hand by the side.

AFTER FIRING TO LOAD FROM THE POSITION OF AIM.

10. LOAD.

One time and two motions.

First Motion. Face to the front, turning on the left heel, carry the right foot forward, placing its heel against the hollow of the left, but without altering the position of the body; bring the piece with both hands to the left shoulder, the barrel to the front, the left hand at the height of the chin, the right hand at the small of the stock, piece detached from the shoulder.

Second Motion. Lower the piece to the ground without shock, place the butt as in No. 1, and carry the right hand to the cartridge box.

TO FIX AND UNFIX BAYONET FROM THE POSITION OF SHOULDERED ARMS.

11. *Fix*—BAYONET.

One time and three motions.

First Motion. Carry the right foot forward, placing its heel against the hollow of the left, but without altering the position of the body; at the same time seize the piece with the left hand at the middle band, detaching it slightly from the shoulder.

Second Motion. Quit the piece with the right hand, and with the left carry it obliquely across the body, and bring it to the ground without shock, resting it against the left thigh, rammer to the rear, butt outside of and against the left foot; drop the piece into the hollow of the right arm, seize the bayonet scabbard with the left hand, raise it as far as the throg will permit, seize the bayonet by the shank and socket with the right hand, so that the lower (now upper) end of the socket shall extend about an inch above the heel of the hand.

Third Motion. Draw the bayonet from the scabbard, turning the clasp towards the body with the right thumb, reseize the piece at the middle band with the left hand, carry and fix the bayonet on the muzzle with the right hand, press the clasp to its position with the right thumb, place the little finger of the right hand on the head of the rammer, lower the left hand to its full extent, without depressing the shoulder.

12. *Shoulder*—Arms.

One time and three motions.

First Motion. Bring up the piece vertically to the left shoulder with the left hand, seize it with the right hand at the small of the stock, and slip the left hand down as low as the chin.

Second Motion. Carry the piece vertically across the body to the right shoulder, change the position of the right hand, so as to embrace the guard, place the right foot beside the left, slip the left hand to the shoulder, fingers extended and joined.

Third Motion. Drop briskly the left hand by the side.

13. *Unfix*—Bayonet.

One time and three motions.

First Motion. Carry the right foot forward, placing its heel against the hollow of the left, but without altering the position of the body; at the same time seize the piece with the left hand at the middle band, detaching it slightly from the shoulder.

Second Motion. Quit the piece with the right hand, and with the left carry it obliquely across the body and bring it to the ground without shock, resting it against the left thigh, rammer to the rear, butt outside of and against the left foot; carry the right hand to the bayonet, with the right thumb push the clasp against the stop, seize the bayonet at the socket and shank.

Third Motion. Wrest off the bayonet, drop the piece into the hollow of the right arm, seize the bayonet scabbard with the left hand, place the bayonet in its scabbard, seize the piece with the left hand at the middle band, place the little finger of the right hand upon the head of the rammer, and extend the left hand to its full extent, without depressing the shoulder.

14. *Shoulder*—Arms.

One time and three motions.

The same as shoulder arms from *fix bayonet,* No. 12.

TO FIX AND UNFIX BAYONET FROM THE POSITION OF ORDERED ARMS.

15. *Fix*—Bayonet.

One time and three motions.

First Motion. Carry the right foot forward, placing its heel against the hollow of the left, but without altering the position of the body; with the right hand raise the piece four inches from the ground, carry it across the body to the left side, seizing it at the middle band with the left hand, and bring it to the ground without shock, resting it against the left thigh, rammer to the rear, butt outside of and against the left foot.

Second Motion. Drop the piece into the hollow of the right arm, seize the bayonet scabbard with the left hand, raise it as far as the throg will permit, seize the bayonet by the shank and socket with the right hand, so that the lower (now upper) end of the socket shall extend about an inch above the heel of the hand.

Third Motion. Draw the bayonet from the scabbard, turning the clasp towards the body with the right thumb, reseize the piece at the middle band with the left hand, carry and fix the bayonet on the muzzle with the right hand, pressing the clasp to its position with the right thumb, place the little finger of the right hand on the head of the rammer, lower the left hand to its full extent, without depressing the shoulder.

From this position arms can be shouldered as in shoulder arms, from the *fix bayonet*, No. 12, or returned to the position of ordered arms, as follows:

16. *Order*—ARMS!

One time and one motion.

Bring the right foot to the side of the left; with the left hand raise the piece four inches from the ground, and carry it over to the right side; sieze the piece with the right hand immediately below the left, drop the left hand by the side, lower the piece to the ground with the right hand, and take the position of ordered arms.

17. *Unfix*—BAYONET!

One time and three motions.

First Motion.—Carry the right foot forward, placing its heel against the hollow of the left, but without altering the position of the body; with the right hand raise the piece four inches from the ground, carry it across the body to the left side, seizing it at the middle band with the left hand, and bring it to the ground without shock, resting it against the thigh, rammer to the rear, butt outside of and against the left foot.

Second Motion.—Carry the right hand to the bayonet, with the right thumb push the clasp against the stop, and seize the bayonet at the socket and shank.

Third Motion.—Wrest off the bayonet, drop the piece into the hollow of the right arm, seize the bayonet scabbard with the left hand, place the bayonet in its scabbard; seize the piece with the left hand at the middle band, place the little finger of the right hand upon the head of the rammer, and extend the left hand to its full extent without depressing the shoulder.

From this position arms can be shouldered as in shoulder arms, from the fix bayonet No. 12, or returned to the position of ordered arms, as in No. 16.

18. *Inspection*—Arms !

(*With bayonets unfixed.*)

One time and three motions.

First Motion.—Carry the right foot forward, placing its heel against the hollow of the left, but without altering the position of the body, with the right hand raise the piece four inches from the ground, carry it across the body to the left side, seizing it at the middle band with the left hand, and bring it to the ground without shock, resting it against the left thigh, rammer to the rear, butt outside of and against the left foot. Drop the piece into the hollow of the right arm, seize the bayonet scabbard with the left hand, raise it as far as the throg will permit, seize the bayonet by the shank and socket with the right hand, so that the lower (now upper) end of the socket shall extend about an inch above the heel of the hand.

Second Motion.—Draw the bayonet from the scabbard, turning the clasp towards the body with the right thumb, re-seize the piece at the middle band with the left hand, carry and fix the bayonet on the muzzle with the right hand, pressing the clasp into its position with the right thumb, then seize the head of the rammer with the thumb and forefinger of the right hand, the other fingers closed, the elbows near the body, draw the rammer as in *Draw Rammer* No. 5, and let it glide to the bottom of the bore.

Third Motion.—Bring the right foot to the side of the left, with the left hand raise the piece four inches from the ground, and carry it over to the right side ; seize the piece with the right hand immediately below the left, drop the left hand by the side, lower the piece to the ground with the right hand, and take the position of ordered arms.

19. *Inspection*—ARMS!

(*With bayonets fixed.*)

One time and three motions.

First Motion.—Carry the right foot forward, placing its heel against the hollow of the left, but without altering the position of the body; with the right hand raise the piece four inches from the ground, carry it across the body to the left side, seizing it at the middle band with the left hand, and bring it to the ground without shock, resting it against the left thigh, rammer to the rear, butt outside of and against the left foot; seize the head of the rammer with the thumb and forefinger of the right hand, the other fingers closed, the elbows near the body.

Second Motion.—Draw the rammer as in Draw Rammer No. 5, and let it glide to the bottom of the bore.

Third Motion.—Bring the right foot to the side of the left; with the left hand raise the piece four inches from the ground, and carry it over to the right side, seize the piece with the right hand immediately below the left. Drop the left hand by the side, lower the piece to the ground with the right hand, and take the position of ordered arms.

20. THE PRESENT FOR INSPECTION.

One time and one motion.

As the Inspector approaches, the soldier presents his piece, by throwing it up with the right hand and seizing it with the left, so that the little finger rests upon the lock plate, the left hand at the height of the chin, the lock to the front, barrel to the right and opposite the left eye, muzzle inclining to the front.

The officer having inspected it returns it to the soldier, who will seize it with the right hand immediately below the middle band, and bring it to the position of ordered arms. The soldier will stand fast until the officer returns the piece of the next man on his left, when he returns from inspection, as follows:

21. THE RETURN FROM INSPECTION.

Carry the right foot forward, placing its heel against the hollow of the left, but without altering the position of the body, with the right hand raise the piece four inches from the ground, carry it across the body to the left side, seizing it at the middle band with the left hand, and bring it to the ground without shock, resting it against the left thigh, rammer to the rear, butt outside of and against the left foot, seize the end of the rammer with the thumb and forefinger of the right hand, the other fingers closed, the elbows near the body.

Return Rammer, as in No. 7.

Return to *ordered arms,* as in No. 16.

22. *Spring*—RAMMERS!

The same as *inspection arms,* No. 19.

Return—RAMMERS!

The same as the *return from inspection,* No. 21.

23. *Stack*—ARMS!

One time and three motions.

First Motion.—At this command number *two* of the front rank will pass his piece to the left, and seize it with the left hand immediately below the middle band, and with the butt outside and four inches above the left foot, bayonet shank opposite the right shoulder, the rammer to the front, he will hold his piece inclining to the right. Number *two* of the rear rank will raise his piece four inches from the ground, turn the rammer to the left, and pass it to number *two* of the front rank, who will seize it with his right hand immediately below the middle band, incline it slightly to the left, and place the shank inside of, and resting on the shank of his own piece, rammer of the right hand piece to the left, butt about four inches from the ground. Number *one* of the front rank will raise his piece, turning it so that the rammer is to the right, and incline the piece to the left, and in front of the pieces held by number *two;* hook the bayonet shank on the crotch formed by the junction of the pieces held by number *two*.

Second Motion.—Number *two* of the front rank throws his right hand piece directly to the front, places the butt of his left hand piece outside of and against his left foot. Number *one* of the front rank at the same moment places the butt of his own piece between his feet; both abandon their hold of the pieces at the same moment, and resume the position of soldiers without arms.

Third Motion.—Number one of the rear rank passes his piece to the left hand, turning the barrel to the front, places the butt on the ground between the feet of number *one* and *two* in the front rank, and rests the piece against the stack.

24. *Take*—ARMS!

One time and one motion.

At the first command number *two* of the front rank will seize the odd piece and pass it to number one of the rear rank; at the second command number *two* of the front rank will seize his own piece with his left hand, and the piece of number two of the rear rank with his right. Number *one* of the front rank will seize his own piece with his right hand; number *two* of the front rank raises the stack, brings the butts together, and thus unlocks the stack, passes his right hand piece to number *two* rear rank, and changes his own piece from the left hand to the right. Each man will then take the position of *ordered arms*.

THE RIGHT ABOUT.

Remarks.—The directions for the *right about*, contained in the U. S. Infantry Tactics for 1861, being exceedingly indefinite, it is advisable to execute it, as follows:

Right about—MARCH!

The command *march* will be given while the left foot is raised, but before it reaches the ground. The soldier will plant the left foot, but without bringing up the right foot to the side of the left, will face about, turning upon the balls of both feet, and step off promptly with the left foot in the new direction.

www.ingramcontent.com/pod-product-compliance
Lightning Source LLC
LaVergne TN
LVHW011121110826
845150LV00008B/2214

* 9 7 8 1 4 1 8 1 9 6 3 1 8 *